# A CHIPMUNK'S INSIDE-OUTSIDE WORLD

# A CHIPMUNK'S INSIDE-OUTSIDE WORLD

by Kay Cooper

**Photographs
and drawings
by Alvin E. Staffan**

JULIAN MESSNER    Ⓜ    NEW YORK

Published by Julian Messner, a Division of Simon & Schuster, Inc.
1 West 39 Street, New York, N.Y. 10018. All rights reserved.

Text copyright © 1973 by Kay C. Watt
Photographs and drawings copyright © 1973 by Alvin E. Staffan

Printed in the United States of America
ISBN 0-671-32565-5 Cloth Trade
      0-671-32566-3 MCE

Design by Marjorie Zaum

Library of Congress Cataloging in Publication Data

Cooper, Kay.
A chipmunk's inside-outside world.

SUMMARY: Chronicles the growth of a chipmunk
from birth to mating.
1. Chipmunks—Juvenile literature. [1. Chipmunks]
I. Staffan, Alvin E., 1924-    illus. II. Title.
QL737.R68C66    599′.3232    72-11958
ISBN 0-671-32565-5
ISBN 0-671-32566-3 (lib. bdg.)

*For my parents, Jack and Margaret Cooper*

ACKNOWLEDGMENT

The author acknowledges the kind assistance and advice of Dr. John R. Paul, Curator of Zoology, Illinois State Museum, Springfield, Illinois.

**O**n the first day, there was darkness. The eyes saw nothing; they were tightly shut. Yet behind the eyelids, the eyes rolled back and forth in their sockets, and the eye muscles grew stronger.

The sweetness of the grassy inner earth filled the burrow and air rushed rapidly in and out of the pea-sized lungs. The creature was only two and one-half inches long. His tiny legs stretched, relaxed, and stretched again, pushing against the grass-lined nest. But the small ears, curled shut, did not hear the sounds of body movement.

Now there came to the little animal a feeling of warmth from his mother's body. He snuggled against her, burying his pink, hairless body in her fur. In that moment, he squeaked softly. The little animal seized his mother's nipple and swallowed a drop of warm milk. This was his first food.

He fell asleep. It was in May of the year and the male chipmunk was one day old. He was one of five baby chip-

munks born in the underground burrow.

Four weeks passed, and it was June.
The male chipmunk, marked like his
brothers and sisters, was almost six
inches long from his tiny nose to the
tip of his tail. His soft fur was colored
the brown of autumn leaves. On his
rump and thighs the brown color
turned rusty. His underside was
creamy white and his feet tan. The
five dark and two white stripes run-

ning down his back were so straight that they seemed to be painted on.

Light stripes, bordered by dark markings, ran above and below his eye. A dark streak passed across his eye. A black spot marked the back of his nose.

Now his rounded ears had unfolded and his brown eyes, which were mostly pupils, had opened. On each front foot were four toes with claws and a small thumb covered by a soft, rounded nail. Each hind foot had five clawed toes.

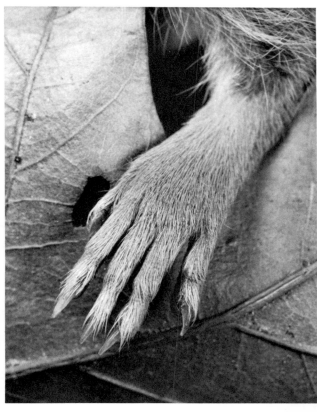

During these weeks, only the mother chipmunk was with her babies in the burrow, which was located in a wooded hillside. The father chipmunk had left the mother before the babies were born. This was the female's first litter.

Usually a litter averaged four or five babies, but it can contain as few as one or as many as eight. A female chipmunk's gestation period was about thirty-one days. She had one or two litters a year, during April or May, and July or August.

By mid-June, the male chipmunk resembled his parents. His flattened tail was almost three inches long and the hairs were colored tawny. Three dark stripes, one down the middle and two near the edges, ran through his tail. The chipmunk used his tail to balance himself on tree branches and to express emotion. He might hold his tail straight up when excited or frightened.

Sometimes he jerked his tail when excited.

His nose, ears, and eyes had become so keen that he could detect those creatures he instinctively knew were his enemies. His slender forepaws, equipped with strong, curved claws, could dig large holes in the earth or hold the smallest of seeds.

Twenty teeth had grown inside his mouth. The front teeth were used for cutting and gnawing, while the side teeth were used for chewing. A member of the squirrel family, the chipmunk

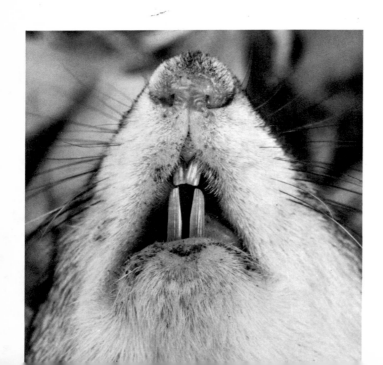

was related to mice, rats, beavers, and hamsters. All these animals were called rodents. This meant that the large incisors, or front cutting teeth, never stopped growing. The back of the incisors was softer than the front part, so the back edges wore away faster. Because of this process, the rodent's teeth were kept sharpened when he gnawed hard food, like corn and nuts.

On swift feet, the chipmunk scurried about the burrow chambers, where his mother had stored nuts and seeds. The young chipmunks no longer needed their mother's milk. From the outside world, she brought such soft foods as mushrooms, berries, snails, and tender plant stalks, for them to eat.

When eating a nut, the chipmunk sat on his strong hind legs and let his forepaws hold the nut. Quickly he

stripped the nut coat with his sharp front teeth and chewed the food with his side teeth.

The chipmunk had two cheek pouches, one on either side, with the openings on the inside of his cheeks. The pouches extended from his jaw-bone down into his neck. They were like the pockets on a shirt. The chipmunk could stuff his pouches with food that he carried from place to place. Sometimes he used his pouches to carry dirt.

Squealing and nipping, the chip-

munk tossed playfully with his brothers and sisters, rolling over them in the burrow. By doing this, his muscles and body were being strengthened for life in the outside world.

In late June, it was time for the chipmunk to leave the burrow. Sun beams streamed into the burrow's entrance, luring the chipmunk from his earth-dark nest. More and more he was

drawn nearer the sunlight until, early one morning, he pattered to the burrow's entrance, peeked out and was gone.

Outside, the plant life surrounded him on all sides. Maple, oak, and sycamore trees appeared dark and huge in the woodland. Instantly the chipmunk's rounded ears caught the sound of the whispering beech leaves blowing

in the breeze. Spiderworts and bell-
flowers dotted the woodland floor.

The chipmunk scurried through
the wet grass. The grass blades bent,
and their dew drops fell where a
daddy longlegs walked. Somewhere
above, a cardinal whistled a loud tune.
A black-capped chickadee, riding atop
a swinging tree branch, repeated a
brisk little *chick-a-dee-dee-dee*.

The chipmunk darted down the wooded hillside, holding his tail straight out behind him as he ran. First he stopped at a stream for a drink of water. Then he lay almost flat on the ground, scooting across the woodland floor on his stomach.

Slowly he crept forward, keeping his entire body close to the ground. He buried his head and nose in the ground litter and sniffed for food. Suddenly he jumped twice and caught a frog. Hungrily, he ate the animal. He liked the taste of the frog, and chuckled in delight. Even with his mouth full, he could call and make noises.

Most of the time the chipmunk was silent. He usually made noises

only for a reason. His most common call was a loud *chip*. This might be sung for many minutes. When angry, he barked violently *chuck-chuck*. He might give a trilling *chipp-r-r-r-r* if frightened or alarmed.

The chipmunk continued his search for food, traveling in short jumps, and covering a foot of ground in a single leap. At the end of each jump, he sniffed the ground for food. Again and again he leaped and searched the ground. Then suddenly he froze.

Huddling close to the ground, he wrapped his tail around his hindpaws and hugged his chest with his forepaws. His nostrils twitched. His ears and eyes were alert. He was trying to catch the slightest sign of food or an enemy. He remained motionless for several minutes before continuing his search for food along the woodland floor.

Far above, a blue jay sailed over the chipmunk. The bird carried a mouthful of tender young insects to her babies. All year, the jays would alert chipmunks and other animals in the area to the approach of any stranger. When the chipmunk heard the jays' loud screams of *jay, jay, jay,* he stood on his hind feet and checked for any signs of an enemy.

In the fall, the blue jays would split nuts open with their sharp beaks. Some of the nut pieces would fall on the ground. The chipmunk and other animals would find and eat these pieces.

Perhaps ten feet from where the chipmunk moved was a decayed oak stump. Its bark, once hard and rough, had become soft and brittle. Piles of crumbling wood lay on the ground providing a habitat for earthworms, millipedes, and insects. Such animals were food for the chipmunk. By eating insects, the chipmunk helped to reduce

some insect populations which were harmful to crops. Most of his diet, however, consisted of berries, seeds, and nuts.

There were also holes in the stump, which had been drilled by woodpeckers in search of insects hiding in the wood. Such holes would be good lodging places for nuts gathered by the chipmunk in the fall. During periods of mild winter weather, the chipmunk might return to these lodging places for food.

For many weeks now, this stump had been a favorite resting spot for many kinds of wildlife, including several chipmunks. At this particular moment, a towhee was resting there. All year, the bird brought seeds to the stump. One seed would drop into the thick mass of moss and fungi which blanketed one side of the stump. In time, a tall tree might grow, its many roots creeping down the stump's sides into the soil. Then the threading roots might smother the stump and provide a protective place for chipmunks to hide and to build their burrows.

With each day, the chipmunk's trips from the nesting burrow became more and more frequent. He wandered farther and farther along the wooded hillside.

As nature had planned, he was becoming more independent. He darted down the bank to a stream with his brothers and sisters, then scurried off by himself. He sniffed the air to the right and the left, and he sniffed the ground, always searching for food.

When he passed rocks or stumps, he looked for places to hide. During the chipmunk's lifetime, he would cover about an acre of ground and would always need good places to hide from enemies. In good habitats where there was plenty of food, water, and shelter, one acre might support four to fifteen chipmunks. Chipmunks living in areas where there was little food, water, and shelter might have to cover as many as three acres in order to survive.

During the hottest part of the summer, the chipmunk's burrow served as a refuge from the sun. For long periods each day, he slept with his family in the cool, dark burrow. He emerged only in the early morning or late afternoon.

On these outings, he often encountered other chipmunks and together they hunched on their hind legs atop a rock or stump. Then they would raise their voices and almost drown out the music of singing birds with their rapid chipping sounds. Some birds were even attracted to the singing chipmunks.

One day the chipmunk journeyed to an oak tree along the wooded hillside. Suddenly a fox squirrel raced down the tree. For a moment, he stood before the chipmunk. Then he whirled

around and scurried up the tree. The chipmunk stared after him with slow-blinking eyes. Instinctively he was not afraid of the squirrel.

The fox squirrel ran down the oak, turned about, and dashed up the tree again. This time, the chipmunk followed him.

Quickly his legs carried him forward to the tree. The small body turned upright and his claws dug into the tree's corky ridges. There was strength in those legs to lift his furry body off the ground, to climb higher and higher into the tree. Swiftly, he pattered across a rough branch, swinging his tail from side to side to keep his balance.

High in the tree, he heard the squirrel chattering. But the chipmunk paid no attention.

Before him was a red-eyed vireo's nest. He entered the nest and turned around on the eggs. The adult birds cried and flew above him, trying to drive him off the nest. For a moment the chipmunk looked at them. Then he cracked one egg shell with his teeth. Eagerly he lapped up the creamy egg. When he finished, he moved headfirst down the tree to the ground. The squirrel, still in the tree, chattered after him, but the chipmunk ignored the noise.

He sped through the undergrowth, whisking between grass blades and squirming between small vines. He was halted abruptly, as the vines around his body tightened and hung there. Alarmed, he called a trilling *chip-r-r-r-r*. He tried to pull away, but the vines held him tightly. He jerked harder and the vines broke. They slid down his hind legs and he was free.

This was the chipmunk's first experience with an enemy — ground ivy. He did not know that some chipmunks become entangled in certain vines and finally die.

The chipmunk rested and then walked slowly through the vines, out of the undergrowth. Leaning on his strong hind legs, he sat up straight. Then he cleaned himself, as he did several times a day.

Rapidly, he licked his forepaws with his tongue. Then he ran his paws, which were wet with saliva, over and over his face until the fur laid flat and moist against his skin. Lowering his head, he stroked his white stomach with his tongue. Then he twisted his body around and pointed his head down to one side. Again he moistened his fur. He did not stop

until all parts of his body, except an unreachable spot between his back shoulders, were wet.

At last, he cleaned his tail. Holding it with both forepaws, he brushed the length of the tail. The tail gleamed in the sun and the chipmunk stared at it. The moist hairs winked at him. The chipmunk ran.

The summer sun had just shown its red-orange blaze on the last day of August, when the chipmunk stopped returning to the nesting burrow. He was about three months old, and he had started to dig his own burrow.

Seeking a secluded spot, he dug under some tree roots on a hillside. Such places as a wooded hillside, log heap, stone pile, broken rocky ledges, or shrubbery made good sites for chipmunk burrows.

As the chipmunk worked, he threw the dirt behind him like a dog digging a hole. The chipmunk dug straight down for almost a foot, on a more gradual slope for about three feet, and then — below the spot where frost was likely to reach — he formed a long straight passageway. He extended this several feet, making it only two inches wide, so he could just squeeze into it. Such a passageway helped to aerate the soil and to provide for rain and snow run-off.

Now and then he pushed away a heap of dirt with his nose and fore-

head, his front paws extended on each side of his face. Moving like a miniature bulldozer, he didn't stop pushing until all the dirt was removed from the opening. Sometimes he packed his cheek pouches with dirt and dumped it outside the burrow.

Next, he hollowed and scooped the storage chambers. Some chipmunks might have as many as four chambers. One of them — located in the lowest part of the burrow — might serve as the area for storing nut shells, seed husks, and body wastes. Toward the rear of the burrow, he fashioned a sleeping area

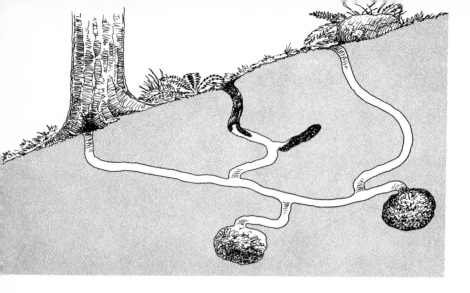

about a foot wide and a foot high. The other two chambers would serve as storage areas.

Next year, the chipmunk would dig new storage areas and passage-ways, and make new entrance holes. Some of these entry holes, plugged with dirt and debris, would not be used very often.

After digging for several days, the chipmunk completed the chambers and tunneled gradually upward to make a second exit into the outside world. Because he dug the second opening from below, there was no pile of dirt around it — no sign which might reveal the burrow's presence to an enemy.

The chipmunk sniffed the hole and scratched the ground with his forepaws. Then he scampered to the burrow's mouth and sniffed around it, smelling the earth. A pile of dirt remained around the hole. Alarmed, the chipmunk's tail shot straight up, and he sniffed the air for a scent of an enemy but sensed nothing.

For long minutes he remained motionless. Finally, he used the dirt to seal the hole and carried leaves and bits of grasses to the entrance. He placed them carefully over the spot.

But the chipmunk was still alarmed. He scurried to the burrow's back opening, and covered the hole with weeds and grasses, to hide it even more from his enemies. Now his burrow had one well-hidden entrance that had once been a second opening. Only the chipmunk knew where the plugged-up hole was, and he could open it if he ever needed it.

While the chipmunk was building his burrow, a young gray fox worked on the same hillside, digging a den in the earth. Chipmunks, mice, and rabbits were his diet.

The hillside also hid another burrow. Last year, this particular burrow had belonged to a woodchuck, but a weasel had adopted it this year. The weasel was probably the chipmunk's most dangerous wild enemy.

The chipmunk, busily working away, did not know how close his enemies were. The long, slender weasel could squeeze into the chipmunk's burrow and dig out the plugged hole. The weasel could also climb trees, so the chipmunk could not escape from him by scurrying up one.

On the ground, the fox could catch the chipmunk. He also could dig into the burrow, but not fast enough to come near the chipmunk.

But the chipmunk's burrow was well hidden in the hillside and, therefore, it served as a refuge from the weasel and the gray fox.

When returning to the burrow, the chipmunk did not follow the same path he had followed the last time he came home. In this way, he did not make a visible trail to his burrow's hidden entrance.

Once while the chipmunk was searching for food in the outside world, the wind caught the scent of a cat and brought a warning to the chipmunk. Instantly, he dashed back to the burrow in high, leaping bounds.

In early fall, when the ground was covered with nuts and seeds, the chipmunk made little deposits of food under bushes. He especially liked nuts with thin shells such as beechnuts. Before placing the food in his pouches, he carefully bit off the sharp points of the nuts and seeds.

Darting under a bush, he dug out a small hole with his front claws. Quickly, he spilled in the food by squeezing his pouches with his paws. He added a little dirt and a few pieces of grass and twigs to hide his supply from other animals. Before winter, he would return and open up his storage places.

Now safe in the burrow on a hot autumn afternoon, the chipmunk's quivering nostrils smelled the musky odor of a snake. The young animal had sniffed this odor many times in the outside world, but never before in his burrow.

What the chipmunk did not know was that this particular blacksnake was about ready to shed his skin, and his entire body had taken on a ghostly appearance. His eyes were milky and fogged by this growing process. Temporarily blinded, the blacksnake sought

a refuge until his skin had been shed.

The snake did not detect the chipmunk until he slid into the burrow.

The chipmunk reacted first, warning the intruder with a rapid *chuck, chuck, chuck*. Terrified, the chipmunk darted to the second exit. He could not stay in his burrow now.

The snake glided toward him. The chipmunk had to unplug the hole quickly. He pushed wildly at the dirt with his front paws and forehead. The earth would not give!

The snake slid closer, his odor mingling with the musky smell of the chipmunk. The chipmunk was still pushing when the snake struck his right hind leg. The painful bite gave him that extra push which drove the packed earth upward into the outside world. In an instant he was free.

Hurt and scarcely able to move his hind leg, the chipmunk dragged himself to a group of rocks. He felt the rough surface of the rocks bouncing beneath his body, hurting his leg even more. He dropped off the rocks into a small crevice. Hidden by the rocks, the dazed chipmunk lay still.

It seemed the pain in his leg would never stop. The minutes crept into hours before the chipmunk moved. First a slight trembling swept through his body. Then he slowly moved his legs and felt pain in the injured one. He could still move it, but the muscles were torn and bruised.

Slowly he licked his leg, his saliva cleaning the wound.

Now a gnawing hunger twisted inside his body. Painfully, he pulled himself away from the rocks. Nearby he found an ample supply of blackberries. He climbed upon a log to reach the food. His leg ached.

For long minutes, he gulped down the berries, letting the juices pour down his face, making it all black and blue.

Later, he returned to the rocks. In his new home, he would be safe until he was able to dig another burrow.

For days the chipmunk remained hidden in the rocks. He only emerged to eat the berries and to lick the dew off the plants.

In the evenings, he was greatly alarmed. Never had he experienced the nighttime excitement of the outside world. During those hours, he had always sought the safety of the burrow.

Above him in a large sycamore tree, a screech owl was wailing his shivering cry. By sitting still, the owl resembled part of the tree and was not seen by larger owls. Tonight, he was watching for mice on the ground. Surely if the owl could have seen the chipmunk in the rocks that evening, he would have swooped down and killed him.

Near the rocks a skunk was on the prowl, also searching for food. She turned over bits of bark and small pieces of debris and ate the crickets and roaches she uncovered. But, like the owl, she was hunting for mice and larger prey to ease her hunger pains. Tonight a chipmunk would make a good meal.

Along a nearby stream moved a raccoon. Although not one of the chipmunk's usual enemies, a raccoon would eat almost anything he could find, and a chipmunk was a welcomed change in diet. As the raccoon waded into the cool water, he turned over stones, looking for crayfish. Later that night, he crossed the rocky ridge where the

chipmunk slept. He did not sense the smaller animal.

A week had passed since the snake entered the chipmunk's burrow. Once the chipmunk returned to his burrow. But he smelled the snake's odor around the entrance, and was afraid to enter the burrow. He turned back to the rocky ledge.

By now the chipmunk had become a little thin, and his fur seemed dull. Although his leg still ached, it had healed nicely. He returned to those places where he had deposited nuts and seeds, opened them, and eagerly ate the food.

However, most of his time and energy was spent fulfilling one desire —a need for shelter. Selecting a wooded hillside as a site, he had the new burrow dug before the first of October.

Now the chipmunk prepared for winter. Busily he crammed his cheek pouches with food. Stuffing one pouch and then the other, he brought in a load of more than two tablespoons of food at a time to his underground storage areas.

The chipmunk never selected damp

food like berries or mushrooms, so nothing ever decayed. His stored food stayed dry.

In late October, the chipmunk had the storage chambers packed with food which he would eat during the winter and spring. In the sleeping area, he made a nest by laying broken twigs and grasses over a lumpy pile of nuts and seeds. When winter came, the chipmunk only had to awaken long enough to reach under his sleeping area for food.

In November, when only the shriveled, brown leaves clung to the oaks, the chipmunk stayed in his burrow for long periods of time. Outside, the sun hung low in the sky. Cold air swept across the ground and drifted into the tunnel, chilling the chipmunk.

Then one morning a cold, creeping fog poured over the outside world.

Frost twinkled on the grass blades. Winter was coming to stay. The chipmunk entered the burrow and plugged the entrance with leaves and packed earth to keep out his enemy, the weasel.

Sealed inside the earth, the chipmunk settled into the sleeping area and rolled himself into a tiny ball. Breathing a little sigh, he wrapped his tail under his legs and up over his nose. Then he was still. His breathing became quiet, quieter. His heart pumped slow, slower.

Now, as in his babyhood, there was the darkness, the silence, and the grassy sweetness of the inside world. The chipmunk drifted into a deep sleep. The warmth of the inner earth and his own body heat would keep him from freezing. Above him, the

outside world turned colder as the sun blinked dim rays of light across the sealed entrance. It began to snow.

On warm winter days, the chipmunk woke up, ate, and then fell asleep again inside the dark burrow. Only thirst brought him outside in icy weather to lick the snow for water.

About the last of February or the first of March, the winter sleeping period ended. The chipmunk scampered across the woodland floor searching for seeds and nut pieces that he had not yet eaten. In severe weather, however, the chipmunk stayed in his burrow and slept on the crisp, dry nest.

In the spring, the chipmunk was a mature adult, weighing about four ounces and measuring almost a foot long from the tip of his tail to the tip of his nose. He pattered from the burrow and looked for a mate. The first female he met was sitting on a stump, but she did not seem to be impressed by him.

Becoming excited, he held his tail high and flicked it back and forth. The female jerked her tail and dashed

away. The male followed, caught up with her, and the two rolled over and over in the grass. Then they mated.

A few minutes later, the male and female parted and went their separate ways. When they met on occasion that spring, the female was no longer friendly. She ruffled her tail, chattered, and chased the male away.

Late in May, a litter of four chipmunks was born in an earth-black burrow. Above the nesting chamber, the soft rains of May soaked the thin

new oak leaves and filled the woodland streams. Spring was everywhere,
providing the chipmunks with water,
food, and shelter. Now the outside
world was ready to support new life
and to welcome the first scamperings
of the newborn chipmunks.